Praise for *Upon Waking*

"These brilliantly lyrical affirmations in the poetry of Kitty Costello reveal that the soul of the streets of San Francisco is among the freest and most defiant in the world. Her truths overturn the deceit of our times. A triumph for the People."
Jack Hirschman
Emeritus Poet Laureate of San Francisco

"Costello could have called this collection Songs of Experience if the title hadn't already been taken by William Blake. Her voice is wise, warm, conversational and dark—a good combination for poetry."
Tamim Ansary
Author of *West of Kabul, East of New York* and *Destiny Disrupted: A History of the World through Islamic Eyes*

"A seam of joy and resilience runs through these poems. The journey from mythic and Christian territories through more political landscapes and on to Buddhist renewal is a transmutation worth traveling through."
Dawnine Spivak
Author of *Grass Sandals: The Travels of Basho*

"A sense of loss, wonder, and beauty throughout... some really stellar writing here."
Eric Robertson
Author of *Whatever Comes of Not Knowing*

"Kitty Costello's profound and beautiful poetic journey, *Upon Waking*, is the kind of poetry we need in these times—poetry to keep us real, sane, hopeful, while also mirroring our aching hearts. Poetry that opens our senses.... Poetry that takes us into heartbreak, then lifts us into a lyrical lightness with a dash of haiku, a whirl of sweetness, and a wondrous stretch of words...."
Thanissara
Author of the book-length poem *The Heart of the Bitter Almond Hedge Sutra* and *Time to Stand Up: An Engaged Buddhist Manifesto for Our Earth*

Upon Waking

New and Selected Poems

1977–2017

Kitty Costello

© 2018 Freedom Voices Publications
All Rights Reserved.

FREEDOM VOICES

P.O. Box 423115
San Francisco, CA 94142
www.freedomvoices.org
orders@freedomvoices.org

Distributed by:
AK Press, 370 Ryan Ave. #100, Chico, CA 95973; akpress.org

Some of these poems have appeared previously in—

The Dean Lipton Memorial Anthology,
San Francisco: Grow Like Weeds Press, 1993

Goddesses We Ain't, ed. Lucy Bledsoe,
San Francisco: Freedom Voices, 1992

Image and Imagination, ed. Ben Jess Clarke,
San Francisco: Freedom Voices, 1997

Sangha News, San Francisco Insight Meditation Community,
San Francisco: Winter, 2014

Street Spirit,
San Francisco: May, 2013

Tender Leaves,
Tenderloin Reflection & Education Center, 1990-1996

Womanblood: Portraits of Women in Poetry & Prose,
San Francisco: Continuing Saga Press, 1981

ISBN: 978-0-915117-28-4
Library of Congress Control Number: 2018906063

Cover art: "Clayton's Laundry Pole" (34th St, Oakland, California),
a watercolor by © 2018 Elinor Randall
Author photo by Jo Babcock

For my beloved parents and teachers.
I lucked out.

TABLE OF CONTENTS

Acknowledgements — 8
Preface — 9

JOURNEY — 11
The Other — 13
Journey — 14
Tetons — 15
Hau'ula Haiku — 16
Aftershocks — 17
Sentience — 18
The Work He Must Do — 20
Rebirth — 21
Reading Cold Mountain — 22

INVITATION — 23
Invitation — 25
Secrets — 26
Menarche — 27
Offering — 28
Anima — 29
Archery — 30
Cure — 31
<u>Your</u> Poem — 32

TAPROOT — 35
The "M" Word — 37
Grandmother Haiku — 38
Holy Saturday — 40
Easter Mourn — 41
the watched god — 42
The Second Leaving — 43
Our Father — 45

PREPARATIONS — 47
Overview — 49
Vet — 50
Nine Haiku For A Locked Temple — 51
To Fast Eddie — 52
Blindspots — 54
Overview 2 — 55
Thirty-Nine Haiku For Manuel Babbitt — 56
Preparations of a Warrior — 60

NOCTURNE — 61

Haiku	63
Dream of the Hermit Card	64
Dream of the Bear	65
Nocturne	66
Somewhere Beyond the Rain	67
Dream on Easter Morning	68
Old Moon	69
My Old Friend, the Dark	70
Spring Equinox Dream	72

TRIBUTES — 73

Elderwoman	75
For Alya	76
The Writer's Vigil	77
My Prayer for You	78
Small Poem	80
Chant for Going Home	81
Too Soon, Carlos, Too Soon	82
Grief and Loss	83

PLAY — 85

How to Simplify Your Life in Ten Easy Steps	86
Haiku	87
Housecleaning Haiku	88
Out of the Hat	89
Siren Song	90
Picking Procumbens (Blackberries)	92
Haiku	93
Ode to the Pelvis	94
Being a Full-on Genuine All-the-Way *Poet* Poet	96

UPON WAKING — 99

No Self	101
I Mind	102
Impermanence	103
Fierce Grace	104
Meditation Hall Haiku	105
Marana Sati	106
Dedicating the Merit	108
Last Day of Retreat	110
Upon Waking	111

About the Poet	115

Acknowledgements

For encouragement and wise feedback on early versions of this collection, deep gratitude to dear writer friends Eric Robertson, Doug Childers, Kathleen Au, Paul Bloom, Kimi Sugioka and Dawnine Spivak. For feedback and support on later drafts, many thanks to Clifton Ross, Jess Clarke and Maketa Groves.

And to my other longtime writing companions who have welcomed and inspired me all along the way—Aline O'Brien, Chrys Rasmussen, Mary TallMountain, Leonard Irving, Alfred Robinson, Margot Pepper, Gayle Markow, Anita Kline, and Thanissara. Much appreciation.

Deep gratitude to writing teachers Jack Sheedy, Carole Klein, Diane diPrima and Sandy Boucher, for guidance, rigor, modeling, and for showing me how to access the creative wellspring within.

Immense appreciation to my music mentor Toby Tate, for insisting on improvisation and original composition, for showing me where skillful practice can lead, and for teaching me that music is everywhere.

Many thanks to Dean Lipton and Tamim Ansary for their sage and tireless leadership at the San Francisco Writers Workshop, and to all my fellow writers there.

Special thanks to the women of the original Tenderloin Women's Writing Workshop—Mary TallMountain, Salima Rashida Raheem, Maria Rand, Marsha Campbell, Martha Nichols, Elisa DeCarlo, Myrnalene Nabih, Carolyn Krantz, Virginia Blair, Caroline Heller, Anna Sears, Lucy Bledsoe and all the others. What a feast of truth-telling, inspiration and support!

Much gratitude to Hedgebrook women's writing retreat for radical hospitality, for rich community, and for nurturing women's belief in their own voices.

Deep appreciation to Jess Clarke and Art Hazelwood for layout wizardry. And to Beth Saunders Stanford and all the activists, artists, writers and editors who have kept the mission of Freedom Voices Publications vital for more than a quarter century.

A hearty thank you to Elinor Randall for her artwork and for inspiring me to live a more adventurous, authentic and anciently-rooted life.

And special gratitude to my husband, Jo Babcock, for steady support and feedback, encouraging me to take my time so I could do my best.

For all these dear ones, and for any I have inadvertently left out, deep bows and blessings to all.

Preface

These poems are gleaned from writing done during the forty years I have lived in San Francisco. They are arranged by theme rather than chronologically, though there are more early poems at the beginning of the book. Sampling from the various sections may give the best overall flavor of subject and voice included here.

Themes of dreaming and awakening pervade this collection. I have recorded my dreams for more than forty years, embracing the shadowy images and unexpected wisdom that emerge from those fertile depths. At the same time, I have cultivated waking practices to access these same deep realms—journaling, hypnosis, meditation, active imagination, visualization—practices I like to call "dreaming while awake." Many of these poems emerged from this ongoing dialogue between waking and dreaming consciousness.

"Waking up" can mean psychological and spiritual awakening. It can also mean waking up from individual and shared delusions—like prejudice, denial of death, the distressing state of our planet, or the hidden costs of privilege and power. Grappling with difficult realities like these through poetry is a starting point, a way to turn toward hard truths with a tender heart… then to begin to ask the question—upon waking, then what? What then?

It is my hope that these poems may bring you, the reader, some measure of enjoyment, encouragement and insight. May we all awaken together.

Journey

The Other

She speaks a foreign language
She has no lips
I hear her voice
but not with my ears
She fills me, surrounds me
but I cannot find her

I envy her; I mock her
She does not mind
I demand a duel
She will not fight
I say she haunts me
She knows the truth

I reach for her
and she runs away
I offer my soul
She cannot be bribed
I let go of her
and she is with me always

She guides me everywhere
though I claim the credit
She knows what I've forgotten
now that I've grown so young
I meet her in my sleep
She dreams me.

Journey
(at Mount Tamalpais)

Here in this spot
in mountain meadow
I travel, standing still

Stones return
to where they used to lay
a thousand years back
I meet every animal
who ever made this place
home,
hear the footsteps
of every human who ever
walked here

Perched where Old Ones
once peered out to sea
I unlearn geography, astronomy—
stars no longer gaseous masses
burning light years off,
but magical gems
dancing weightless on nothing,
painting pictures
for my eyes only
The sea once again
drops off to nothingness
right over the edge

If I am still and silent
I will feel the earth tremble
I will hear the approach
of the dinosaur
his tail dragging behind him
through the ravine.

Tetons

Near Swan Lake
secreted behind low boughs
we wait

A moose ventures
silently into the water,
dips her face
into the cold universe
of quench and munch,
lifting white chin whiskers
as cascading sheets of water
slow to droplets
again and again
each time she straightens
chews, surveys, then lowers
her long face once more,
persisting far longer than
the telling takes here

A clatter of geese rises,
sounds an alarm
for dangers unseen,
then rustles back
into silence of lake sheen

A woodpecker hammers his tree
while beavers on break
stretch sunning atop the beginnings
of a new lodge, now just inches
above the water line

A tiny gasp fills me—
"Oh! This!
This is the world!"

Hau'ula Haiku

Morning tea brewing
Counting haiku syllables
Five, seven and five

On sunrise beach walk
dancing through sudden breaker
lava bites my toes

Just beneath the waves
deep in coral cluster homes
jeweled fish abound

Grandma selling fruit
calls, "Coconut! Young like me!"
Machete hacks down

Ceaseless rain and wind
Content to sit, go nowhere
gazing out to sea

Nestling deep inside
in timeless, drenched afternoon
my animal self

In wind rustled palms,
in every crashing wave
ancestor voices

Aftershocks
San Francisco, October, 1989

We peek out windows over the city,
say Hold still, City, don't fall!
in the tiniest whisper
so that nothing will tremble
not another brick come loose
not another overpass crack
No more entombing of life
Oh please!
pass over us this night

Or else
    Move, Great Earth
        Find us
           Touch us
              Rock us
                  Keep us
       Our cradle is
           falling
       falling

In my mind is a rubble
I cannot clear
The air is too still
Each buzzing fly sounds
like something else about to happen

              (Between concrete slabs
        beneath wooden beams
              they are trapped right now
           in cracks too small
              for a human being
                  Don't even breathe!)

Set everything on the floor
Put the sky above your head
Wear your shoes to bed
Be ready to tumble
Earth is being reborn.

Sentience

Wind awakens
flutters tree leaves
shimmies trunks
hurries clouds along

Her invisible fingers dance
each grass blade to the root
Her wide arms wrap
round both sides
of nearby mountain

Every cricket call and foot fall
every stormbreak and sunburst
every holler, hush and gale,
record themselves in this living
tablet of mind,
this library of flesh
housed somehow
in bony skull
of impermanent me

Closed eyes move within
track a lone fly
buzzing around my head
as if this creature were
a lesser library of being,
as if this same knowing
did not animate
its gem-faceted eyes
which are at this moment
directing a landing atop
this hair I call mine

Oh how weightless
the storehouse of one self's
lifeknowing must be…

Wind slams a door open
Mind returns once again
to the ever-so-gradual demise
of the one who birthed me

a kiss long-ending.

The Work He Must Do

He pushes the sun down behind the horizon
wondering if what he's done is… right,
wrenches caverns in the earth with his bare hands
to make way for the whole ocean

In merciless lava, in nightmare he comes
gleaming in the finely-honed edge of the battlesword,
in the teeth of the tiger ripping warm flesh
is the work he must do

He is the man tilling, turning the soil
uprooting a thousand living things
with a trembling sadness in his heart
He knows the pitiful frailty of it all.

Rebirth

This room is too small
My head bumps the ceiling
I am packed and ready to move
but oh how I struggle
in the hall
by the door
to emerge

My bags are too heavy
My legs don't work like they used to
I don't know how to go

Outside scares me
It is different
like walking on the sky.

Reading Cold Mountain*

Drums grumble nonstop
in the capital city
Deaf men march

Where shall I lend
my small but mighty might?
To what deity or boneyard
shall I make my deepest bow?
 ... hungering for empty belly
  empty of hunger
 A single bell rings

Shall I keep still?
Retreat to the mountains?
Grab my pen, ink overflowing?
Or let life's canvas
go on scrolling
its vast emptiness?

The cries of the world lament
louder than ever
Sorrow and tenderness
burst beyond any known self
Odysseys and homecomings
may both lead
heavenward or astray

Was there ever
an elsewhere to escape to?
If so, what a tiny portal
it must be by now

If the sage was planning to return,
now would be a good time
Yes. Now.

Han Shan was a legendary 7th century Chinese sage and recluse. He took his name from Cold Mountain, the refuge he called home, where he purportedly left his poems scrawled on the rocks.

Invitation

Invitation

Allow me to paint you a picture
draw you a roadmap
or better yet
take the next path that calls to you
It will lead to a misty place
out on the edge of your vision
flickering elusive like
limbo, like
twilight
In a hidden cove
a secret cave with
fire crackling inside where
old ways meet new ways
dreams merge with day
answers lose their questions
night touches dawn
Deep in thick forest
where elves and gypsies
still roam wild…

How you glimmer
soaring free
slipping lightly
through the heavens
You have been here before
Remember?
Get ready
Soon you will transform
to proper size
Come
There is nothing left to do
but play.

Secrets

In the hollow of a tree trunk
in the heart of the forest
we rest
cradled, hidden

Dark-haired little lass
prances up the path
She seeks a place to hide

We lift the skirt of a redwood trunk
She nestles there
waiting

"Don't tell," she says
We cross our lips

Voices drift up from the riverbed
approaching, advancing

She giggles out from her hiding place
to loving, scolding arms

Echoes recede, drift away
fade off down the trail

Before she vanishes round the bend
she turns to wink and wave
Momma tugs her arm

And they never saw us
no never saw us
They never saw us at all.

Menarche

Walls shedding skin
the flow oozes dark inside
unravel the potential
unbirth

Womb aches open
to the rose
to clay mud
banked thick at riverside

From invisible cord
a universe unties
Birth of next moon
The sun bows his head.

Offering

Let your tears fall from my eyes
sting my cheeks
I can weep in your place

Lean here
This strong arm you've given me
can bear your weight

Let the creature that eats at your heart
call out inside me, cry from my lips instead
until the voice is gone
We'll spit the poison out

When the shadows of vultures
grow on the ground
we will laugh,
no fear anymore

Oh please
don't disappear
to those places you go
in the dark of night
or
if you must
        … disappear

Listen
I have a song for you
It is cool; it is light
Drink as much as you like
until your thirst is gone.

Anima

Could you turn inward
when I touch you
and reach for your inner lover?
I would not steal you from her
She can teach us what is simple

If we could slip ourselves
one atop the other
like a ghost through a wall
the form would fit

She taught you to be born
but then, forgotten,
she seemed like a wish or a choice

You know her…

Archery

Our arrows are always poised, aimed
In another moment one may pierce your heart again or mine—
the bowstring always taut
the quiver never empty
though arrow after arrow has flown and struck its mark

Sometimes they pass clean through
before you know it
There is shock perhaps but no outcry

Then how many times
I've felt it go
so slowly
cell by cell
through the skin
between the bones
to the moist
tender core,
the prey inside
falling where it stands

In time we learned to parry, leap and dodge
We sent incoming arrows sailing far and wide
But later one would regret,
might pick an arrow from the leaves,
try to force it bare-handed through one's own chest

Now the bowstring sings again
Another winged messenger takes flight
I'm proud and sad my aim is true
You are laughing as you fall

This kind of death has come so often
it's shed all thorns of thistly fear
How we yearn now for the wounding when it's gone.

Cure

If we can meet

and find our own dark treasure,

heal our own dark scars,

our hearts will be mending

              cracks in the world.

Your Poem

This is a poem
you are writing for your self,
maybe allowing lids
to cast downward,
an inward gaze,
feeling the be-ing-ness
of this given body

inhabiting belly
avowing heart
allowing upwelling throat

Invite all that is yearning
to be sung or chanted,
sworn to or ranted—
a simple sound universal,
a holy tantrum or primal blessing—
longing by this very next
breath to be made
Listen for it…
You know it by heart

Perhaps in sudden memory
you clutch tight the rails
of a twirling carousel,
cradled in the whole
whirl and spin and ache and
                                weeeeeeee!
of the round round world, or

bumping hard now
into edges
of thick-throated
unspeakables
stuck so long in there
you made a you of it

Tell this. *Tell this!*
no matter its dark, inky threat

Allow the sound
Let loose in real time—
unforeseen arias,
ancestral rumblings,
age-old sighs, or

with trusty pen,
with mighty *h o w l,*
stab through the heart of whatever
vampire needs staking

Then back from ancient history—
Celebrate
this shaft of light bathing the floor,
this hungry cat meow,
this urgent rustle of palm leaves,
this silent, unending
sweep of clock hand

Where is this headed?
You choose particulars,
your free will finally riding
the wave that used to flood you

Reach the shore
Land soggy and astonished
like your first
earthly entrance
Here may you sing
your sojourn's fullest anthem—
the song that always
leads home.

Taproot

The "M" Word

All the 6th grade girls
chased behind me in the playground that day,
crying, "What is it? What *is* it? Tell us! TELL US!"
They knew it was something BIG but they didn't know what.
Who had dared to speak the word in our Catholic school lunchroom
over peanut butter sandwiches and fudgesicles?
Who had said the "M" word?
Was it me? I thought they *knew!*

I run and run in the schoolyard, mortified,
screaming, "Ask your mother! ASK YOUR MOTHER!",
some part of me knowing it was bad *bad* news
for these girls who would, any day now,
have mysterious stains on their panties
or red streaks trickling down their thighs
and no clue why.
They'd think they were going to die!

It seemed so long ago
when I asked my mother about babies,
and without missing a beat
she sat me down at the kitchen table,
roping in my older brother
who had the misfortune to be walking by,
drawing with squeaky chalk
on the blackboard beside the wall phone—
ovaries and tubes and eggs
and blood and sperm and embedded embryos.
My brother glared death ray eyes at me
for getting him stuck in this.
Thankfully for us both,
she left out the part about how
the sperm would find its way into the womb.

And as I ran that day, screaming, "No no no No NO!",
terrified at what the nuns would do if they heard I had told,
I never once thought,
no not even once until this very moment did I think,
they bleed too.

Grandmother Haiku

Older than memory
a crumbling covered wagon
down the farmhouse lane

Small girl left behind
grips prairie grass with both hands
as cyclone rages

Down the homestead trail
a vision of Christ appears
Grandmother is blessed

Just eighteen years old
taught grades one through eight
in a one-room schoolhouse

Before her lessons
first washed lice from school kids' hair
with kerosene

Headstrong suffragette—
"Is there a chance for me?" asked
Grandfather to be

A farm of their own
in Parker, South Dakota
where Mother was born

Stigmata wounds bled
the marks of Christ, of sainthood
on Aunt Elaine's palms

Family farm foreclosed
Dakota roots forsaken
California bound

Side by side, three graves
Grandmother's grandparents lie
beneath windswept plains

Chiding Granddad's diet—
"John," she'd tell him, "you're digging
your grave with your teeth."

Daily Mass a must
Down on her knees praying
for our immortal souls

Recites her poetry
praising Holy Eucharist
Makes me late for school

In old black and white—
grandparents with shrewd smiles, signed,
Just Mother and Dad

My husband and I slept
first night of our honeymoon
in her hometown

Ceaseless winds whistle
past lonely graveyard headstones
The town disappeared

Holy Saturday*

It's Saturday and He's in the tomb now
Tomorrow He will come out
and then He will be here forever
but we won't see Him anymore

The sun is shining too much
and everyone feels they must go outside
So there they are in the park
bored and blinking in the light
The gleam seems cheap, plated
The real sun must be hiding elsewhere
Something inside is vaguely missing
They don't know what or where it is,
just that in some other place or time
it must be storming like hell

The blood is behind the skin
where it ought to be
but today they want to see it
to know for certain.

The day between Good Friday and Easter Sunday.

Easter Mourn
Washington, DC, April 4, 1999
(for the people of Kosovo)

In delicate dawn of daffodils gay
of magnolias blooming full
the choir sings out
Kyrie eleison   eleison
Lord have mercy   mercy

Somewhere between the Credo and Sanctus
around the far side of the globe
a torrent of humans
flows forth from their homeland
spilling out, spilling down,
an ageless rite
of exile and sacrifice
last suppers untouched
the Lamb of God slaughtered
lowered, entombed

Dawn shines with heavenly fire
against an ever-blackening sky
Who is buried and is risen?
Who takes away the sins of the world?

Bird songs fill this far silence
between Consecration and Communion
Are our trespasses forgiven?

Beyond church windows
cherry blossoms drift
relentlessly down.

the watched god
(upon reading e. e. cummings)

i.
caught we are
in this manmade corridor
between heaven and flesh
straining against
imaginary walls
for the way out,
searching with the wrong set of eyes

ii.
is the halo a mirage caused by evening light?
fallacy of some fool's retina?
let me see this soul you say you have—
perhaps a little test, a simple incision
somewhere in the vicinity of the heart, you say?

> *these saints are shysters*
> *what can they want from me?*
> *these miracles are sleight of hand*

iii.
our god is dead!
we perform the autopsy, dissecting the body
demanding answers! conclusions!
we wait by the tomb with microphones
with cameras, instruments and mechanisms
to record the resurrection, proof positive
but the watched god never rises.

The Second Leaving

It could have been God going away
or some claimed a microbe
had snuck its way in from another galaxy
to make a mess of things

It was like this (for one thing):
cells randomly linking up
with no concern for genus
or numbers of chromosomes and producing
monstrous offspring
like mushrooms and salamanders
mating and bearing
scaly fungi that poked
their little heads through the soil
and snapped at flies or
bulbous lizards that waddled around
like umbrellas or 1950's Cadillacs,
toppling over onto their backs
and flailing their legs like bugs then
taking a bite of themselves for a meal
You can take it from there

But that wasn't the worst of it...
No one knew what was good to eat anymore
I mean, the strawberries looked good
but they broke your teeth
and the sun started hanging around
the other side of the horizon
for days on end
while the moon would come up
full one night and new the next
and you can imagine what that did to the oceans
the waters sometimes raging sometimes
perfectly still   waveless   stagnant
the whales floating belly up
the ships stuck out there for weeks
not knowing which way the current might flow next
or which way north was for that matter because

the stars were all scrambled in the sextant—
Cassiopeia sitting in the Big Dipper
the Pleiades all spread out

Yes it could have been God going away
Some said they heard
the door slam shut behind him.

Our Father

He never said his grandfather was a twin named Bartholomew
never told that Bartholomew was a coal miner in West Virginia
after fleeing Irish famine.
No, Dad's people were all small-town, small-farm,
grow-and-can-your-own, fish-in-the-creek-out-back Ohio folk
his dad a machinist on the B&O line.
Not *our* family, black-faced with soot,
scratching a wage in the earth's dark bowels.

How did Bartholomew make that climb from black poison air,
from premature burial in coal rubble?
How did his son, Granddad Rob,
come to the wide fields of Midwest promise?

Men can be so poor at remembering,
so good at clamping down
the shame of harder times,
letting the string break, the pearls tumble, hope
lessly out of context and order

How do I know any of this?
An in-law, cousin Bob's wife, researched,
sent her family history, after Dad was gone.

Then unearthed in Mother's basement
a handful of pictures from a childhood he'd never shown—
Dad at age 2 on a dark doorstep, in a white smudged
dressing gown, looking slightly stunned.
Whose eye is behind that camera?
His own dad, proud of his first born?
1920 or '21, just before the '20s began to roar?

Next time we see him, he's 6 or so,
leaning his head against his mother's right side,
his little sister Peggy
leaning on her left.
Grandmother Muriel stands upright
in a proper ladies' dress and hat,
a Sunday before church perhaps.

he was the candy kid,
goody two-shoes, my mother always said—
obedient, helpful Catholic school boy,
doing his momma's bidding when asked.
Altar boy? No doubt a prerequisite
for his entry into the seminary
which, yes,
he left before becoming a priest,
before becoming Our Father,
who wasn't in heaven,
though according to his beliefs
and by all Catholic measures,
he is now.

No, he was Our Father who art
downstairs in front of the TV with a beer,
or Our Father who gave each of us our first bath,
or Our Father who art behind the camera clicking away,
or Our Father who art at work taking care
of other people's children who need it more,
or Our Father who singeth tenor in church choir,
or Our Father who doth smell so foul after eating
Progresso canned minestrone soup
that we refuse to kiss him goodnight,
or Our Father who art out in the station wagon
smoking his pipe and listening to the ballgame
because Our Mother who art a fussbudget
won't allow that stench in the house,
or Our Father who maketh groan-worthy puns,
or Our Father who doth watch Gilligan's Island
and Gomer Pyle with us downstairs in the family room
while Our Mother art upstairs watching
the slightly more highbrow Perry Mason or Alfred Hitchcock,
or Our Father who art no longer
in the body
in the box
in the ground
in the old church cemetery,
or Our Father who art in heaven
if anyone ever was.

Preparations

Overview

An eagle builds its nest higher
A panda crawls deeper into the forest
    to keep two-leggers from her cubs

A great blue heron touches down near high voltage wires
    suffers stress, begins to lose feathers
    pecks the young ones without thinking why

Another drill pierces another uranium deposit
Some country or other loses something it shot up into space
A crocodile dives deeper to miss the motorboat blades

Some old buzzard salutes himself
    for selling off the carcasses
    he's already picked clean

An Indian waits on death row
A young girl goes on trial for being raped
The soup line moves slowly forward

Metal fatigues in the desert, hottest day in history
World leaders all book facelifts
Another native tribe enters oblivion.

Vet

War within him—
razors and bayonets
grenade blasts and white phosphorous—
threatening to dance down neurons
to his hands and tear
an inadvertent life apart:
a passerby, his wife

Affectionate wrestling
out of the question with those
specters popping up like
rifle range dummies

Thought the woman could cleanse him
while he
loved her, loathed her
loved her…
out of his ears or crown
the ghosts of those
dead by his hands would
vacate, remove their mutilated
bodies from inside his
eyelids where they'd taken up
residence
since 1953

A class war gender war world war
U.N.-sanctioned police action
raged on in his bloody arteries
long after the accords were signed
the bodies were buried
the duped soldiers were back in clean sheets
trying not to commit
a homeland holocaust.

Nine Haiku For A Locked Temple

(After Dorothea Lange's photo "Buddhist Priest Locks Temple," taken in Florin, CA during the roundup of Japanese Americans for internment, 1942)

We come for last prayers,
our few possessions in hand,
find temple doors locked.

                                  No one worships here.
                                  Now even our gods scare them,
                                  trapped liked ghosts inside.

Keep safe this temple,
our faith no shield from terror,
yet not abandoned.

                                  Buddha may find us
                                  locked within prisons of shame,
                                  our priest hauled away.

Prayer beads pass his hands
trace the unbroken circle.
Life is suffering.

                                  If passersby ask
                                  where we have gone, tell them to
                                  ask the government.

Our roots are unearthed
by hands unseen, wrenched up with
clumps of dirt dangling.

                                  Prayers are set loose.
                                  Offerings fill the passing winds
                                  from temples within.

Dreamers dream beyond
clack of train wheels through far lands.
Stillness in motion.

To Fast Eddie
San Francisco, January 23, 1990

I watched you dance your dance of death,
grabbing your blood-soaked shirt
and throwing up your hands,
grabbing your shirt and throwing your hands up again
as the circle of blood grew and grew

You, stumbling into traffic
right across the road patch
where the city hall water main broke last week
flooding the street,
facing us in traffic with a plea we couldn't answer,
falling down and standing back up
falling down and standing back up,
a fierce defiance of your death,
your gestures saying, "My God,
look what's happening to me.
Someone help me. Help!"
falling down and standing back up
falling down…

The road crew watched
like you were just a crazy Black man,
stepping wide to direct
the traffic past your dance,
no one holding you
And yes, you *were* crazy
Who wouldn't be
with all their blood spilling out
from a knifehole in their heart?

And then the dance was done
You were gone from there—away

—the medics cutting the clothes from your breathless body,
trying to jumpstart a heart with a hole in it

A white man in a blue jacket,
all I know of the murderer who escaped
southward down the street

"They ought to get these people out of here,
find a place for them!" says a bystander
who doesn't want a homeless person being stabbed
right where she has to see it

And everywhere tonight I think I see
blood oozing out from under doorways,
white men in blue jackets,
something gleaming in their hands

I go home, shut and lock my door
and pray out over the rooftops
for all of you who have
no door to shut behind.

Blindspots
(the day after Epiphany)

Where we do not want to look
is a tomb we must jump into
a well we must throw ourselves down
with no guarantee of ever hitting water

Pitiful small hands try to push blood
back into heads that are bleeding onto the street
try to push bullets
back into barrels of guns

Not a single voice cries out
as everyone walks the wrong road together
just for the company—
a shifting of bones within skins

The pillows are fluffed up too large
the heads propped away from the bodies
No one monitors the dream world
Some are caught sleeping on their feet

The world fills with synthetic dirt
with plastic aquarium plants
The eyes of fishes swell
Birds unscrew themselves from the sky

And still we walk upright as if everywhere
legs had not been lost to landmines
In bed we somehow still reach
our lips out for kisses

Some eyes break, won't blink
Those few go sane, rise fiercely from the sheets
step straight to the edge of the volcano
and witness the fire
                        without falling in.

Overview 2

We say our prayers at the automatic teller machine,
then swing on down to the espresso drive-thru,
quick to duck those daily driveby hijack shooting-spree
letter-bombing headline hounds

By commercial demand
all music will now be played an octave higher
All speed limits are lifted
Overeating is a new requirement for citizenship

Dreams may be accessed via mind chip
on pull-down menus behind the eyelids;
blink twice on preselected category to open file

Science has shown some genetically-prone
to sleep on concrete in every weather
Wind slices meaner down these city streets
Clouds scrape the sky

In the park the trees overachieve,
strain toward the sun; you can hear
their sap gurgling to a boil
their wood snapping
their seeds pattering down
in all the wrong seasons
No one can remember where food comes from

Now they've built a mini-mall
in the last remaining meadow
Let's stop there for a jiffy-lube big gulp
in a 102-ounce retrashable can
Let's drive a long way to get it

Or better yet, hop a fast plane
from an ever-shortening runway
How much shorter can they get?

Thirty-Nine Haiku For Manuel Babbitt*
Executed by the State of California, May 4, 1999

Manuel Babbitt
Seventeen years on death row
awaiting last day

Brutal murderer
winner of the Purple Heart
inside the same man

In Nam at eighteen
Wounded at siege of Khe Sanh
bloodiest battle

Legs, heads, body parts
for seventy-seven days
flying everywhere

Was med-evaced out
on a pile of dead Marines
Sent back to combat

Worked search-and-destroy
wiping out whole villages
Counted dead after

Survived Vietnam
Carried the nightmare within
Brought war home with him

Lived in a cardboard box
Dodged imaginary bombs
on mean city streets

Thirty convictions—
burglary, armed robbery
Sent to mental ward

First African American to be executed by the State of California since the death penalty was reinstated in 1977.

His homeland haunted—
landmines hidden underground
ghosts that won't lie down

Locked up for two years—
paranoid schizophrenic
Sent back to the streets

Killed an old woman
Robbed and beat and almost raped
in a flashback rage

Leah Schendel died
A grandmother of seven
stolen forever

Half-naked body
found covered with a mattress
Strap tied to ankle

Same method he learned
to shield and ID corpses
War casualties

Took lighter and watch—
an action Vietnam vets
call "souveniring"

In Manny's pocket
his brother found engraved lighter
initialed L.S.

Sacramento cops
assured him Manny'd get help
not a death sentence

His plea: not guilty
reason of insanity
Could not recall the crime

Public defender
a drunk and racist lawyer
ignored war trauma

Felony murder—
a Black man convicted by
an all-white jury

Leah's family
hoped his death would bring them peace
Eighteen years of grief

First Black sent to die*
First time evidence hearing
was ever denied

Eleventh hour
governor and supreme court
reject his appeals

Refused his last meal
"Give it to a homeless vet"
Fasted last two days

Tried to hear last beat
each night as he fell asleep
while he still could breathe

Outside San Quentin
hundreds kept silent vigil
in his last hours

"This is a cakewalk"
says vet friend standing vigil
"He's with the Buddha"

"The hard part's over—
living dead thirty-one years
tormented by war"

Strapped inside "gray wolf"—
his name for the death chamber
Predator scapegoat

The last words he spoke
"I forgive all of you" then
silence echoing

Wind rips through Kansas
through Oklahoma all night
tornadoes raging

He died half hour
past his fiftieth birthday
A candle blown out

Witnesses silent
long after he lay there still
Thumping of old pipes

Doesn't have to wear
a monster face anymore
Forever asleep

"The death penalty—
a form of ethnic cleansing"
his brother proclaims

Feels blood on his hands
For pain he caused both families
he fasts to atone

War never-ending
Add one to the body count
then add another

Preparations of a Warrior

Plunging endless burial grounds
she comes to sing the songs that must be sung
sifts seeds from undersides of lives cut short
tucks corpses in for the long long night, then

sets all rotting worlds aside
leaves them for earthworms who need them
leeches bitterness back into the soil where it belongs
blows her candle out

The edges of the earth move closer

*   *   *   *   *   *   *

At break of day
with one hand raised, the other bound
to sacred entryways of dreams
she caresses the underworld, the stars, ponders
what only all our minds together can hold
This is her prayer

Leaving sentences unfinished, kisses half-done
she unpins her black armband for the last time and
raising the oldest of flags
moves her feet
squarely across battlelines.

Nocturne

Haiku

Awaken late night

counting syllables in dreams

Notebook far away

Dream of the Hermit Card

The traveler bears a lantern
swinging side to side
not to light the path
but to project the image
      the image of a traveler
            walking on a path
        bearing a lantern
      swinging side to side

At night the path stays light
the air a muffled glow
It winds in broad curve
ever upward

By taking the next step forward
the path creates itself
beneath the traveler's feet.

Dream of the Bear

I find myself alone with a faceless man.
We stand before a pond so stuffed with life
I can't believe my eyes—
the water so full of fishes,
the sky so full of birds,
I marvel at how they can swim and fly
without bumping into each other.

Then somehow a bear is killed.
I didn't mean it. I couldn't stop it.
It wasn't my hands
but the hands of the faceless man
who's done the deed and now is gone.

I am left with the bloody carcass.
What do I do with this bleeding,
half-dismembered bear?
It was killed in a bad way—
a death without prayer or heart—
too easy, this death,
like shooting them in their lairs as they sleep.

The bear's death grieves me.
His spirit is thick in the air.
I search my mind for old ways
no one ever taught me.
How do I use his flesh well?
What shall I do with the hide, the bones?

The birds and fishes witness me.
The sky glares down.
And somewhere villagers crouch unseen,
silent in my struggle.

Nocturne

She travels downwind
breathless through the underbrush
circumspect
        wary
Who is the predator?
He never shows his face

Shadows pass by
with no figures attached
She struggles with the night
dodging the invisible

Listen! everywhere!
her name in the wind
Watch! everywhere!
the eternal vigil

The whole earth sighs beneath her feet.

Somewhere Beyond the Rain
Randy's Vermont Farmhouse Guestroom, 12:02 a.m.

Ball jar at bedside
bursts with larkspur and loosestrife
    and a solitary sunflower
A small Buddha with peaked hat
    watches from perch on windowsill
Raw handhewn housebeam underlines
    golden-pine window frame in fine finish
Frilly pinstriped sheets poke out from beneath
    old rose-wool blanket, thick with hair of cats
        in whose territory I now reside

A lone fly buzzes against the ceiling
A lone spider hangs from invisible thread
Across the room a wall of bare lath
    awaits plaster that may never come

Raindrops glisten in webs beyond the windowglass
Rain patters gently on empty fields
Downstairs old Memphis sleeps behind the toilet
    safe from cruel pecks of other chickens
Outside four roosters, three geese and a gander
    nestle blessedly quiet. Somewhere beyond the rain
        horses huddle hidden

Behind the clouds Jupiter and Saturn persist
    rising and traveling the night sky in Taurus—
        clockwork measuring far more
            than the limits of my sleep.

Dream on Easter Morning

The sun has indeed arisen
but in a corner of the sky
a patch of stars still shimmers
against its dark night-curtain

"What could be blocking the sun?"
my sister asks
as my brother and I
pause with her to ponder

Beside us a stair leads
skyward to a house
where our mother and long-dead
father now reside

Poised on the stair
we turn back to see
the dark sky-hole grown now
to gigantic proportions
Stars and planets streak by
helter skelter
leaving trails of light against
cold black space

A small patch of blue still shines
at horizon's far edge
but how long can it last
in this terrible cataclysm
of earth tumbling
headlong, unbound,
cut loose from the sun?
When will this chill air freeze
to eternal night?

Our feet move again upon the stairs
as we begin our heavenward ascent
to join our forebears where they dwell now
up there in what's left of the sky.

Old Moon
(just when we need you most)

Forgetting your phase
we set out in the night alone
No one asks where the 13th month went
No one turns her face to the sky

Now when old ones die
the hole closes over behind them
Who still knows the songs
          to carry them to your dark side
the songs to call them back into our dreams?

We wander off, hapless, in corridors of moonbeams
try to shake the sacred sounds from trees—
          tampering, wakeful—
Who remembers how to sleep?

We are lost!
Come find us!
Teach us how to hear
          the roots drinking water.

My Old Friend, the Dark

How I love the insides of my eyelids,
the shades that shield away the frenzied world
Soon the show begins

Never have I dozed to find
the dream screen broken or empty,
the screenwriters on strike

Each night my old friend *the dark*
dims the houselights
with reverent hush, then

Voila! I shrink to ant-size, explore
the craggy chambers of a small lava rock
that lives on my bedside table

Renowned teachers
I'm gaga over
suddenly seek my counsel

An old boss drives up 40 years later,
no longer a tyrant, but taking me for
a joyride in his slick classic Lincoln

Chased by bandits, I dive whole-bodied
into a tiny sidewalk puddle
and get away clean

An old poet friend makes
the long long trek from the other side
just to advise: *"Read Dylan Thomas!"*

I fly—not your jetliner kind
of whoosh and zoom
but breast-stroking with easy glide

just above the tree line,
something I always knew
deep down I could do

Yes, there's plenty of murder
and everyone having sex with the wrong person
but with no price to pay

My long-dead father listens
on the other end
of the phone…

How could I ever fear *the dark*
when it doorways me to the underworld and back
without yet having to die

No Eurydice needing any
Orpheus to lead her
back to day

This inner sight, a gift at birth
not strived for or earned,
this nightly broadcast for one

No signal
No device
No fee

Just dream.

Spring Equinox Dream

I find myself among
a special order of nuns—
the-sisters-who-have-fallen-from-grace
They have sinned
yet this is their special charm
They are not at all wicked
They are not shunned
Having sex or not
isn't the point
They are holy in a new way

When I fathom who these nuns are
I magnetize
arrive home
among these strong and deep
wise and kind
fiercely forgiving women
… my people.

Tributes

Elderwoman
for Mary TallMountain

She needs only to see
one raindrop
to close her eyes and know
the whole ocean

The rocking chair tells her tales
of where its wood grew tall
The window tells her
who passed by
who peeked through

These shapes are old friends
come to visit
again and again

O how long the years of grief
O how she loved her way back
to the world of wonder

Now she climbs the attic stair
that leads to other times
She merges
with nightsounds of wilderness

She lives at the heart
of the mysteries
laid bare.

For Alya

Side by side in the garden
she shows me the scar,
traces where they took the vein
from inside her thigh
and put it here, inside her heart.
She cannot lift things,
gestures the unimaginable
wound within, the violence done
to save her.

"God wants me to stay
a little longer," she shrugs.

She inspects each flower
and passing bird in turn,
points to a small birdhouse
I've hung in a tree,
traces the route a cat might take
to reach that branch.
"Bird very careful," she says,
letting me know
I haven't got the thing right.

Tells me how daily
she fixes her sight
on the window across the street,
one eye at a time.
"Exercise! Exercise!" she exclaims.
"Not everyone can keep
walking and working!"

She doesn't like
being so still.

Geraniums on their tall stalks
sway back and forth to greet her.
She waves back and says,
"Hello."

The Writer's Vigil
for Dean Lipton, who died April 23, 1992

Where have you slipped off to, my friend?
The earth moved just now, an aftershock,
and I awoke with dreams of you
rumbling and lumbering through the long dark night.
Sleeplessness takes me.
My watch has come.
...

Poems are like dreams while you're awake
I used to say back when.

Dreams?
Dreams were against you, you said—
all tubes and masks and blades
and severed parts that kept you
nightly wakeful and walking,
walking and wakeful until dawn.

Don't call before one, okay? Okay.
...

So I'll see you.
I'll see you then
is what you said when I last phoned
your hospital bed.

When will you see me then?
...

Where have you wandered off to now?
I search. I feel you. I follow you roaming
through the night time streets
down the alleyway of my heartbeat
to the North Beach of my mind—
churning, wrangling, wakeful—
you go wandering on 'til dawn,
fading into the light
in the quiet morning
of your last and deepest sleep.

My Prayer for You
for Allen Ginsberg (d. 4/5/97)

I fold my towels at the laundromat
behind dark glasses,
mismatch my socks,
remember you live, reading
Ode to Plutonium
and reaching up to find
my face wet with tears
I was too rapt
to know I was shedding

Thank you for
unhooking my brain into itself,
for tripping my breath and ear,
for honest tears,
for going feral

I claim you as teacher,
as teacher of my teachers,
as maker of a soulstream
I could jump into

I didn't know
when I was three years old
that you went on trial
for the right to howl,
but the howl was heard for good
and was a sound I could follow
to places worth running away to

You resurrected us from
homogeny, heterogeny,
from garters and girdles and ties,
back into a world that bleeds

Your vision stamped reality
with the pain it really held,
with a lusty laugh
always ready to sound
and echo
          echo

Cracking the stifle,
sounding the alarm,
singing us awake
with small quirks
of lyric and harmonium,
beflowering rifles
saying be don't do,
ranting against
the tabloiding of everything,
going om
          going om

Behind glasses,
full of kisses,
a fury of life,
an agony of candor

Back home I turn the soil
to plant cucumber seedlings
The rectangle of brown earth becomes
a grave I bury the roots into,
the cauldron of death and rebirth
watered with tears—
my prayer for you.

Small Poem
for poet Gary Johnston (d. 1982)

I knew a person once

and then he died

I didn't see him around much anymore

Chant for Going Home
for the scattering of Mary TallMountain's ashes

Now to your home
you are going
To the source of rain
you are going
To *Iliuliuk*
you are going
In Bone Blossom's care
you are going
On a blue note
you are going
In *Niguudzaagha's* canoe
you are going
To the seven seas
you are going
Released from old forms
you are going
To the birthplace of stars
you are going
To your wild birds
you are going
Among vanished tribes
you are going
Through grandmother's root
you are going
Like snowflakes adrift
you are going
Through turning fishwheels
you are going
To the land of the muse
you are going
Scattered on winds
you are going
going.

Iliuliuk: A river in Unalaska where poet Mary TallMountain chose to have her ashes scattered.

Niguudzaagha: Athabaskan word for Great Horned Owl.

Too Soon, Carlos, Too Soon
for Carlos Ramirez, who died March 10, 2013

You could see his halo
from blocks away
down sun-seared Mission streets,
his glow arriving well before
his sweet smile-crinkled face
came to full view

Beside the produce stand one day,
our friendship still new,
he showed me how
you could wrap yourself,
each arm clasping
the opposite shoulder,
to gently knead and rock
rock and knead in self-embrace
whenever feeling
loveless or afraid

Eyes and ears deeply tuned, he'd ask,
"How's Kitty today?" meaning me
and my answer,
rapt in soul listening,
let me hear
unforeseen selves speaking

When powers-that-are
                bellowed,
       leaned their mean weight down—
           soldiers, fathers, petty cops—
he shied deeply in
to ready refuge
of his own vast tenderness

Crooning his poem tunes,
teaching us how
to make rain,
pied pipering children
who let flow for him
their no-longer-silent poet voices
onto once white paper.

Grief and Loss

G	iant incomprehensible web
R	eaching out to you, Mother.
I	nterwoven chords
E	xtending back to the beginning
F	rom before first breath.
A	nother death cannot compare.
N	o ripping of life's fabric
D	eclares itself so deafeningly.
L	etters of alphabets I once spoke
O	nly with you,
S	ounds that make no
S	ense without you to hear.

Play

Simplify Your Life in Ten Easy Steps

Life is complicated

Discipline is overrated

Eat whatever's on the shelf

Let go of the sniping self

Do not try to overthink it

If it smells funky, do not drink it

Give yourself this very breath

Be mightily curious about the moment of death

Rest your feet, rest your head

And when you speak leave something left un…

Haiku

First rains are falling

and me with open-toed shoes

My socks go squish squish

Housecleaning Haiku

I don't mind the grime
Paper piles oppress the most
Ghosts live in them.

―――――――――――

Who put clutter here?
My feet should walk clear and free
Self-imprisonment.

―――――――――――

The dust will be back
no matter how much sweeping
Enjoy the broom swish.

Out of the Hat
(ideas for poems I'll never write)

First kiss
Coming unglued
Exercises in fertility
Lessons on lessening
Unhinging from binging
Ransom for the handsome
Pulling up pants and jumping out windows
The dropping of a dime
Editing out things like poop
Things I never did
Things I wish I never did
Being too young
Being too old
Lifting lids
Pouring forth
Cutting loose
Pulling the plug
Getting ready to pounce
The first thing I saw
The last thing I'll say
Poetic amnesia license
Unexpected springboards
Things that break a fall
Animals inside my skin
Stepping on sidewalk cracks
Recalling what's never been
Making things up for real.

Song

Out in the silent urban night
someone has parked his car
and every time a truck barrels past
a sound can be heard wide and far

It started not as a low deep whine
It rose not to a fury
It slowed down not its steady pace
nor sped up in a hurry

But pulsed away in monotonous blare
a blare that rent the sky
and out from every window perch
the sleepless humans cry

Oh where oh where has the owner gone?
Is he somewhere far away?
Is he tucked in sweet in his lover's bed?
Will he linger long into day?

Or is he near but too full of beer
to bother with the racket?
Is a posse searching for him now
armed with rope and hatchet?

But the sound drones on and the mind takes flight
into trivial minutia—
a Prius? a Ford? an old farm truck?
or a brand new silver Porsche?

But no matter what the cost or style
no matter the miles per gallon
all vehicles are classed the same
when they commence this howling

In dreams we roam the starless night
a mob with torches high
Who knows what form our revenge may take
if we ever find this guy

But then like a missing final step
the hated sound goes mute
We sigh a collective "ahhhh" out loud
call off our fierce pursuit

Each head floats down to its pillow
tranquility restored
We dream sweet dreams in the silent night
… til the blaring starts once more!

Picking Procumbens (Blackberries)

Patiently poking past perilous prickles

picking panfuls of purple pendulous perfection

persistently probing a preponderance of pesky perforators

plucking pure pearls of plump parabolic plenty

pouncing on prized plunder predaceously

partaking of puckery pulp with piggy passion

painting the palate a pulsing prurient pink

purveying a plethora of precious pantry provisions

for prodigious pastries, puddings, purees, parfaits and pies

producing powerful paroxysms of profuse pleasure

prescription for possible portly protrusion

promoting a panoply of ponderous poetry

in perpetuity.

Haiku

Buzzing by my ear

one mosquito through long night

I smack my own head

Ode to the Pelvis

Source of chi, flowing free
Geographic center
where powers leave and enter

Breath can reach down to the base
like a flower held in vase

Rotate, gyrate, swirl & swivel
Half moon bowl
that can twist and roll

Holding tank of fluids filling
Dips and bends and never spilling
Bowel and bladder, fecal matter
Cauldron bubble, source of trouble

Gives support when we are sitting
Earthly anchor unremitting

Holds groin and loin where people adjoin
Haunches pumping, animals humping

or secret shame that has no name

Source of life, passion, strife
Deepest knowing, magic flowing
seeds a'sowing, babies growing

Sturdy floor
supports the core
becomes birth door

Sacrum holding spine to tail
Sacred bone we do regale

Glute max ligament connecting
Iliosacral intersecting
Ball joint thumping while we're jumping
Bowing, flexing, neural plexing

Site of dumping and the drain
Furthest organ from the brain
You're the depths we plumb to delve us
Hail to Thee, O Mighty Pelvis.

Being a Full-on Genuine All-the-Way *Poet* Poet

Would I have to dye my hair purple?
Get all esoteric and manic and tangential?
Parade overly self-revealing facts in lyric litany
to make everyone blush but me?
Would my family roll their eyes
even more than they already do?

Must I quit my day job?
Get on SSI?
on the wrong side of the law?
Have sex willy nilly
or not at all?
Should I smash my computer?
write my poems on leaves?
in the sand?
or at least refuse to own a cell phone
Would I forget to brush my teeth?

Must I lose sleep because
great lines just won't stop coming?
Or wear way too much
black eye makeup to readings
get hooked on tobacco again
seduce a priest?
Then repent
eat nothing but rice cakes and celery stalks
and refuse all modes
of mechanized transport

Shall I don a beret at Trieste?
Or eat at St. Anthony's and sing at Glide?
Or better yet, move to Oakland
grow dreadlocks
recite my poems to multitudes
of strangers on the BART

or be a hermit poet
no one ever sees at all…

*   *   *

Or shall I make my poet vows thus—

To wear a halo inside my head
Yield to the shadow
See best in the dark

Turn mind into a time machine
Go everywhere
Be totally present

Reel in really really big fish
from really really deep down
Throw fish back

Know the craft:
Grant readers' every wish for
(fill in the blank)

Lose faith
Get faith back
Stay open no matter what

Sneak past mind
to arrow the heart
with truth we can bear after all

Speak the magic words
Have something real to say
when someone dies.

Upon Waking

No Self

Fell asleep a thousand times

Woke up a thousand and one

but who's counting?

I Mind

I am weary of my mind

It wants without permission
makes my hands
throw things down my gullet
taxing stomach and bowels
with no consultation at all

It and blocks and ducks
before I can even
get a look at what's coming

Takes recess when deadlines loom
Keeps working when lights are out
Holds forth with dubious critique
at all hours

Jumps future to past to future
rehashing what never was
rehearsing what never can be

Gets caught in tomorrow morning's bridge traffic
pines for postcards from those long dead
wails long after sirens have passed

I mind.

Impermanence
for cousin Mickey

As soon as a being wobbles up onto new legs
she begins her fall, slow motion or fast
to meet the ground
All story ends here, horizontal
the cord untied
the puppet strings sheared clean

Seed, stalk, trunk, branch, leaf
limb, arm, flesh, sap, soul
ripening ripely, then
ashes ashes
we all fall down
Every last sigh heaves, irretrievable—
tumble to follow

Some fall in doorways,
on roads,
the traffic stopped
Others fall unheard in woods
alone   away   far
meshing with earth
unseen

A language no longer spoken
a library burned down
a tale that lives on only in someone's mind
a vanishing someone,
or a name rarely thought of at all
a tribe of one
gone home

Rock-a-bye baby
on the treetop
The bough is laden
the weather uncertain…

Fierce Grace
for Ram Dass

Open my life now
like a book being written
in the trees before
paper is born

Bring on the seasons of grace
like well-worn shoes
on new-born feet

Let me trip on my laces
laughing to the bone
all judges overthrown

Breathe me the smoke
of time's ardent fire,
whispered through the fleshy
cave of my passing

Sail my dreams
on updrafts of morning's birth
fluttering their tales
of awakening

Drown me in the untapped brew
Mix all metaphors
in a fine bubbling stew

Rest me here nestled
wreathed in thistles and down
of endless tangible now

Shine the coal of my starless sky
with the radiant cloth of night.

Meditation Hall Haiku

Buddha statue smiles
Wonder what's not on his mind
Are we so funny?

Perched on its cushion
empty bell holds only air
Utters not one sound

Small bug on wood floor
tries to squeeze into a crack
just a wee bit tight

Writing haiku in hall
In silence of company
one burst of laughter

Quick rain after drought
Water drops cling to each branch
All drenched equally

Looking out window
in the dark of night I see
poets reflecting

Marana Sati
(the Buddhist contemplation of death)

At that one single moment
each cell released from every other
unhooked from every marker or perch
relieved of duty
                relieved

letting go the scrambled
anthive of being
no need to tell
the soldiers or scouts
homebodies or queens
the lay of the land
                vigilance let down

Corpse pose:
the eyes recede
easy and deep behind the lids,
sunken in sockets,
the face no longer struggling
with its PR campaign

the jaw come loose
the tongue retired from its duties
ears no longer tuned
to the station of the living
the arms done with labor—
reaching, holding, pushing, praying
no more
the palms no longer
radiant

the legs fall endlessly open, apart
sinew unwinds

the whole sky peers into
the umbilical core
of this former being
nakedness left far behind

all that was once
authored and composed
now decomposing

No self here
Life gone beyond.

Dedicating the Merit*

This is no mistake
You earned your seat
The ride will not be smooth
or if it is, you'll get bored
so let it be
                as bumpy
        as it is

The hardness just is
The loss too
It's a package deal for the journey
none of us signed up for

Your body will be
your best companion
                  until it isn't
              then stay tuned

Everywhere you turn
your attention to receives
the grace of self-blessing:
your broken arm or heart
your unstuffed teddy bear
Keep the list going
It's endless
in light of incessant
injury, puzzlement, churn

May it go easy
in every
possible
way
without going flat

May it go easy for
your children, your dead,
for the person at the party
that you don't want
           to get stuck talking to

May it go easy for
your 7th grade math teacher,
for your poor
doggie who gobbled 9 macaroons

May the delights outnumber
the vexations
May healings abound

and if they don't come
as fast as you would wish,
may you be so so so
kind to yourself while you're waiting

May you remember kindness
May you remember kindness
May you remember kindness.

A Buddhist tradition for sharing the blessings of our practice with all beings.

Last Day of Retreat

Silence yet unbroken

On dining room window

a heart drawn in frost

Upon Waking

I. Down There, Up Here

Two-winged bird of *dreams*—
        sometimes a screeching mayday of befuddli
            a vain pageant of high flung unreacha
                or a mucky dive into thickening soup
  More often
        the scoop   clean truth blown alive
            a fully full cup of cleanest water
                if we can only find the dawn
        without spilling a drop

Then *waking life*—
        sober eyes open wide
        to light-of-day obvious
        cut and dried
        good ol' reliable real life
  or?
        only solid-seeming, one more illusion
                to wake up from,
      make-believe forevers
            falsifying the space between
              here
                    and gone

And don't get me started on advertisements, intoxicants
            newstream and blue screen
        asleeping us in broad daylight, installing
            cherished delusions
      we soon must grieve

...kening

...irst
                inhabit the underworld
      Then—
         climbing the long pathway
                  from down under
              to the sky—
look both ways
(in and out)
read the signs   twice
use your palms
take notes
leave footprints
keep some mud on your shoes
make sure your shadow follows you
bump the edges of the known world
and when you need further guidance

        consult those who came before
             and laid down forever
      They say

Awaken to fragility
              to going… going… going… going….
      Awaken to disavowed selves masquerading
              behind others' crooked smiles
      Awaken to privilege's price,
            you inadvertent predator
            you self-judging prey
Pray
Know hankering from hooked
      Awaken to the whole
              wide
          aching
                gorgeous
            world
      and kiss goodbye

III. The Difference

Know the trail   coming and going
        Traverse often
                Find the moon at noon
If people say, "Aw, you're dreamin'," you'll say,
                      "You bet. It's how I wake up."

Rest often
    but keep moving
        and above all, ask:
            Am I dreaming now?
                Am I awake?

About the Poet

Kitty Costello is descended mostly from potato-famine refugees who fled Ireland in the 1860s. Farmers, teachers, herdsmen, machinists, coal miners—they settled mainly in the Midwest, in Ohio and South Dakota, where her parents were born.

Costello was born in Washington, DC. Her earliest years were spent in rural Maryland on the grounds of an institution where her social-worker father took care of people with extreme physical and mental disabilities. She was schooled by the Sisters of Notre Dame at Catholic University's grade school in DC. Then public school rounded out her education, as did the upheavals and uprisings of the civil rights and anti-war movements in the 1960s and '70s.

Moving to San Francisco in 1977, she worked for thirty years for the San Francisco Public Library, while also practicing Shaolin kung fu and working as a teacher, an editor, and a social justice organizer. She earned a master's degree in social psychology, specializing in labor and mental health, and in recovery from trauma. She currently has a small psychotherapy practice and leads meditation, writing and tai chi classes.

Ongoing participation in local writing communities has been essential to her writer's journey and sparked many of her most cherished lifetime friendships. She is literary trustee for native Alaskan writer Mary TallMountain. She created a library archive for the 70-year-old San Francisco Writers Workshop, and she is writing a history of that group. Working with Freedom Voices, she has helped give voice to marginalized writers and artists, especially in San Francisco's Tenderloin District, for nearly thirty years.

Costello lives with her husband and three cats in San Francisco's Mission District. This is her first collection of poetry.

CPSIA information can be obtained
at www.ICGtesting.com
Printed in the USA
FSHW011316281018
53261FS